What's on MyPlate?

A Guide to Good Nutrition

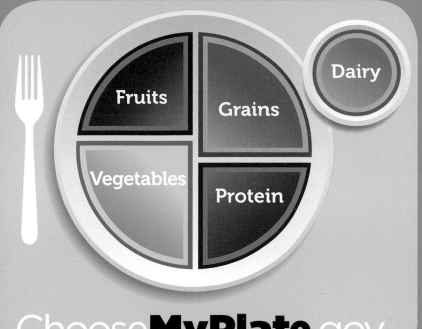

Fruits

Grains

Dairy

Vegetables

Protein

ChooseMyPlate.gov

By Slim Goodbody

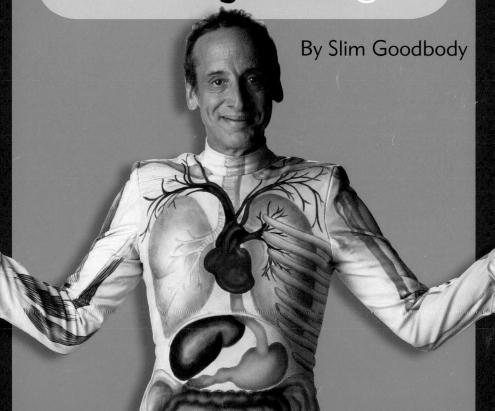

Developed and written by: John Burstein

Designed by: Tammy West, Westgraphix.LLC

Photos: ©Chris Pinchback, Pinchback Photography,
istock, and Shutterstock images

ISBN 978-1-887028-63-9

Contact Information:
Please visit our website at: www.slimgoodbody.com and
at www. healthcurriculum.org

Slim Goodbody Corp.
PO Box 242
Lincolnville Center, ME 04950
207-763-2820

About the Author
John Burstein (also known as Slim Goodbody) has
been entertaining and educating children for over thirty
years. His programs have been broadcast on CBS, PBS,
Nickelodeon, USA, and Discovery. Over the years, he has
developed programs with the American Association for
Health Education, the American Academy of Pediatrics, the
National YMCA, the President's Council on Physical Fitness
and Sports, the International Reading Association, and the
National Council of Teachers of Mathematics. He has won
numerous awards including the Parent's Choice Award and
the President's Council's Fitness Leader Award. Currently,
Mr. Burstein presents his multimedia live show "Bodyology"
in cities across the country.

Choose**MyPlate**.gov

Table of Contents

Words that are in **bold** type appear in the glossary.

MyPlate

Walk into any supermarket and look around. There are thousands of different foods to choose from!

With all those choices, it's easy to feel confused. Which foods are really best for you? What **combination** of foods will keep you the healthiest?

The design of MyPlate lets you know three things right away.

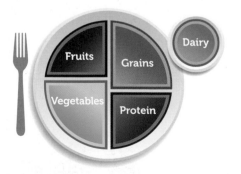

1. You need to combine food from five different food groups at each meal.

2. Even though you need food from all five groups, you don't need the same amount from each group.

3. Fruits and vegetables fill half the plate. This tells you that half your meal should be made up of foods from these two groups.

Food for Thought

Variety is a key part of a healthy diet. Not only do you need different groups of food, you also need to eat a variety of foods within each group.

A Little Chemistry

Before we go any farther, I'd like you spend a moment thinking about three questions:

- **Why do people need to eat foods from different food groups?**

- **Why isn't it enough just to fill up on one kind of food?**

- **Why can't you eat just one kind of food from each of the groups?**

The answer to these questions has to do with **chemistry**. Foods contain nutrients. A nutrient is a chemical your body needs to live and grow. When the food you eat gets digested, it is broken down into nutrients.

Different nutrients help your body in different ways.

Some nutrients help build strong teeth and bones.

Some nutrients provide your muscles with energy to move.

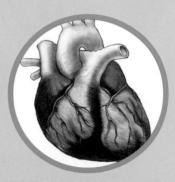

Some nutrients help your eyes see better.

Some nutrients protect your heart.

Some nutrients help your skin heal when it is cut.

Some nutrients help your **cells** fight disease.

Food for Thought

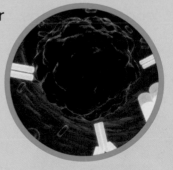

Every food contains a slightly different combination of nutrients, even foods within the same group.

7

Team Nutrient

There are six kinds of nutrients. To stay healthy, you need all six kinds of nutrients on your team everyday.

CARBOHYDRATES fuel your body. They give you energy to get things done. You get carbohydrates from foods like bread, potatoes, rice, spaghetti, fruits, and vegetables.

PROTEINS are your body's carpenters. They build and repair your cells. You get protein from foods such as meat, eggs, and beans.

FATS provide energy that your body can store up for later use. You get fats from foods such as vegetable oil, peanuts, butter, salmon, milk, and cheese.

MINERALS come from the earth. Some minerals add great strength to your bones and teeth. Another mineral helps red blood cells carry **oxygen**. Almost all the foods we eat contain minerals.

VITAMINS help direct the flow of nutrients through your body. They also keep your eyes and skin healthy, help cuts heal, and help protect against **infections**. There are vitamins in almost all the foods we eat.

WATER helps **transport** all the nutrients through your body. There is some water in all the foods you eat, even bread and meat!

Food for Thought

Most foods contain a number of nutrients. But no food contains all the nutrients you need.

Fabulous Fruits

The fruits group includes every fruit in the world, and every 100% fruit juice drink.

Fruits come in many colors. The color is based, in part, on the mix of nutrients the fruit contains. Eat fruits with all the different colors each week. Then, you will be sure to get a wide range of nutrients.

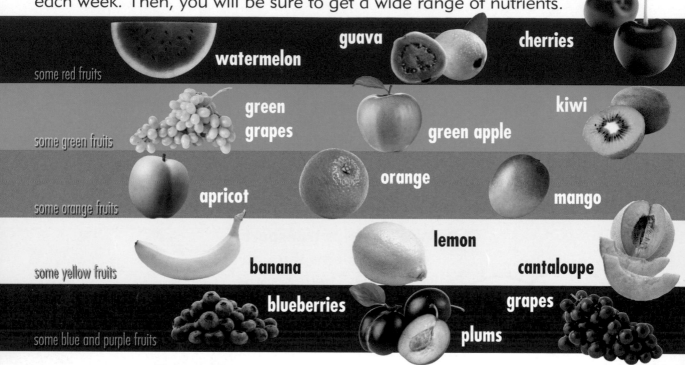

some red fruits — **watermelon** **guava** **cherries**

some green fruits — **green grapes** **green apple** **kiwi**

some orange fruits — **apricot** **orange** **mango**

some yellow fruits — **banana** **lemon** **cantaloupe**

some blue and purple fruits — **blueberries** **plums** **grapes**

EVERYDAY

You can easily include fruits in all of your meals.

You can eat bananas on cereal or blueberry pancakes for breakfast. You can drink a glass of apple juice with lunch. You can snack on an orange or some raisins after school. You can eat peaches for dessert after dinner.

How Much?

You need at least 1½ cups of fruit every day. Since you don't usually eat fruit from a cup, here's a helpful way to think about getting the amount you need:

Each day, eat one fruit (or fruits) from the ONE CUP LIST.
Each day, eat one fruit (or fruits) from the ½ CUP LIST.

ONE CUP LIST
1 small apple
1 medium orange
1 mango
2 large plums
1 medium grapefruit
1 large banana
32 grapes
1 pear
2 halves of canned peaches
1 slice of watermelon
8 large strawberries
1 cup of 100% orange juice

½ CUP LIST
½ large banana
4 large strawberries
½ pear
½ glass of orange juice
1 small container of applesauce
1 plum
½ small apple
1 box of raisons
½ orange
½ mango
½ grapefruit
16 grapes

You can mix and match any way you like. You can pick 1 small apple and ½ pear, or one small apple and 1 plum. You can pick 1 glass of orange juice and 1 box of raisons. It is easy and fun.

Food for Thought

It is very important to wash fruits before eating them. Be sure to rub them well with your hands under clean, running water to rinse away dirt and **germs**.

Fruits of the World

Fruits grow all around the world. The same kind of fruit can even grow in many places.

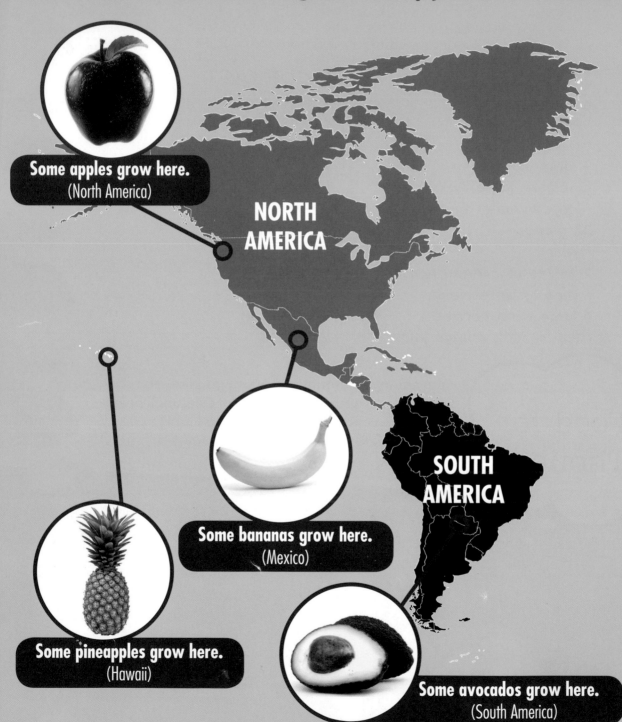

Some apples grow here.
(North America)

NORTH AMERICA

SOUTH AMERICA

Some bananas grow here.
(Mexico)

Some pineapples grow here.
(Hawaii)

Some avocados grow here.
(South America)

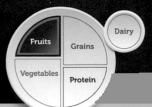

Some figs grow here.
(Italy)

Some pomegranates grow here.
(Egypt)

Some apricots grow here.
(China)

ASIA

EUROPE

AFRICA

Some passion
fruit grow here.
(Australia)

AUSTRALIA

Some mangoes grow here.
(India)

Some papayas grow here.
(Kenya)

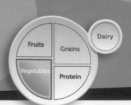

Vital Vegetables

The vegetables group contains every vegetable that grows, along with every 100% vegetable juice drink. Vegetables can be divided into 5 smaller groups, based on the nutrients they contain. Try to include vegetables from the following groups each week.

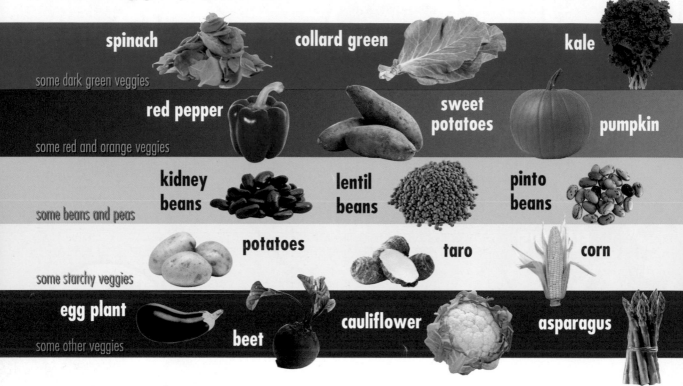

spinach   **collard green**   **kale**

some dark green veggies

red pepper   **sweet potatoes**   **pumpkin**

some red and orange veggies

kidney beans   **lentil beans**   **pinto beans**

some beans and peas

potatoes   **taro**   **corn**

some starchy veggies

egg plant   **beet**   **cauliflower**   **asparagus**

some other veggies

EVERYDAY

You can easily include vegetables in all of your meals.

You can drink a glass of carrot juice at breakfast. You can have a salad for lunch. You can snack on some celery after school. You can have vegetable soup with dinner.

How Much?

Children who are four to eight years old need about 1½ cups of vegetables a day. Girls who are nine to thirteen years old need two cups every day. Boys nine to thirteen years old need 2½ cups of vegetables each day.

You can use these two lists to help you get the vegetables you need.

Each day, eat something from the ONE CUP LIST
and something from the ½ CUP LIST.

ONE CUP LIST
12 baby carrots
1 large bell pepper
1 large sweet potato
1 cup of cooked spinach
1 medium baked potato
3 medium spears of broccoli
1 cup of vegetable juice
1 cup of cooked bean sprouts

½ CUP LIST
6 baby carrots
1 stalk of celery
5 broccoli florets
½ acorn squash
1 cup of raw green lettuce
1 palm-sized piece of tofu
½ cup of vegetable juice
1 small pepper

Food for Thought

Raw vegetables contain more nutrients than cooked vegetables. The reason for this is that heat destroys some nutrients. So, it's a good idea to eat some raw veggies each day. Just be sure you wash them well before eating.

Vegetables of the World

Vegetables grow all around the world. The same kind of vegetable can even grow in many places.

Some sweet corn grows here.
(North America)

NORTH AMERICA

Some yams grow here.
(Caribbean)

Some sweet potatoes grow here.
(Central America)

SOUTH AMERICA

Some squash grow here.
(South America)

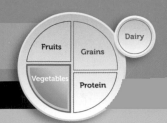
Some kale grows here.
(Europe)

Some beets grow here.
(Europe)

Some rhubarb grows here.
(China)

Some kale grows here.

EUROPE

ASIA

Some eggplant grows here.
(Japan)

AFRICA

AUSTRALIA

Some gourds grow here.
(India)

Some okra grows here.
(North Africa)

Some cucumbers grow here.
(Australia)

Great Grains

The grains group includes all foods made from wheat, rice, oats, cornmeal, barley, rye, or other cereal grain.

All grain foods are not equally healthy. To understand why, you need to know a little about how grain grows. A grain seed has three layers:

The outer layer is called the bran. The main layer is called the *endosperm*. The smallest layer is called the germ.

A grain seed has three parts.

bran

endosperm

germ

If all the layers are used when grain is made into food, we call it *whole grain*. Some examples of these foods are whole wheat bread, brown rice, oatmeal, and popcorn.

If two layers are left out and only the endosperm layer is used, we call it *refined grain*. Some examples of refined grains are white bread, corn flakes, spaghetti, and white rice.

Whole grain foods are healthier than refined grains because they contain more nutrients. At least half of the grains you eat each day should be whole grains.

EVERYDAY

You can easily include grains in all of your meals.

You can have a bowl of whole grain cereal in the morning. You can have a tasty pita sandwich at lunch. You can snack on some crackers after school. You can have some whole wheat macaroni for dinner.

How Much?

Children who are four to eight years old need about 5 ounces of grains each day. Girls who are nine to thirteen also need 5 ounces. Boys nine to thirteen years old need 6 ounces each day.

Since we usually don't weigh our food on a scale before eating, here is a list of what counts as an ounce:

1 slice whole wheat toast
½ an English muffin
1 "mini" bagel
1 pancake
1 small tortilla
1 cup of cooked pasta
1 small biscuit
  (2 inches diameter)
1 small piece of corn bread
  (2 ½" x 1 ¼" x 1 ¼")
1 small muffin

5 whole wheat crackers
½ cup of cooked cereal
  (such as oatmeal)
1 slice of white bread
1 cup of whole grain cold
  breakfast cereal
½ cup of cooked brown rice
1 hamburger bun
3 cups of low-fat popcorn
½ cup of cooked of pasta

Food for Thought

Foods that are labeled with the words "multi-grain," "stone-ground," "100% wheat," "cracked wheat," "seven-grain," or "bran" are usually not made from whole-grains!

Grains of the World

Grains grow all around the world. People use those grains to make different kinds of food.

Some oatmeal is made here.
(Canada)

NORTH AMERICA

Some grits are made here.
(Southern USA)

Some tortillas are made here.
(Mexico)

SOUTH AMERICA

Some cassava bread is made here.
(South America)

Fruits | Grains | Dairy | Vegetables | Protein

Some croissants are made here.
(France)

Some pasta is made here.
(Italy)

Some black bread is made here.
(Russia)

Some soba noodles are made here.
(Japan)

EUROPE

ASIA

AFRICA

Some rice noodles are made here.
(China)

AUSTRALIA

Some chickpea falafels are made here.
(Israel)

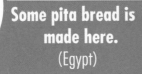

Some pita bread is made here.
(Egypt)

Some English muffins are made here.
(Australia)

Powerful Protein

The protein group is huge. It contains many different kinds of foods with a lot of different nutrients.

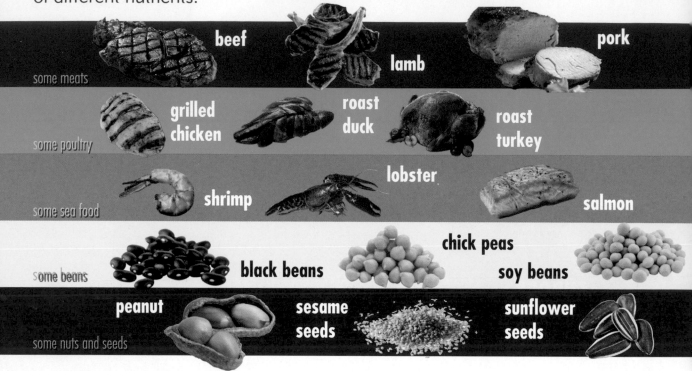

some meats — beef, lamb, pork

some poultry — grilled chicken, roast duck, roast turkey

some sea food — shrimp, lobster, salmon

some beans — black beans, chick peas, soy beans

some nuts and seeds — peanut, sesame seeds, sunflower seeds

Here are some tips about eating well from the protein group:

Try to eat seafood at least twice a week as your main protein food.

Try to include beans, peas, or soy products in your meals as often as you can.

Make sure the meat you eat is lean. Lean meat does not have a lot of fat in it.

You can have a nutty cereal for breakfast. You can have a chicken sandwich for lunch. You can snack on some peanut butter after school. You can have a fish taco for dinner.

EVERYDAY

You can easily include protein in all of your meals.

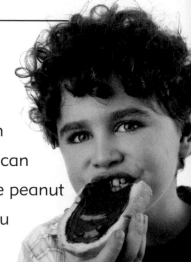

How Much?

Children who are eight years old or younger need three to four ounces every day. Children nine years old or older need five ounces.

Here is what counts as 1 ounce:

1/3 small lean hamburger
1 slice of turkey
1 small handful of nuts or seeds
1 egg
1/3 can of tuna fish
1/3 small chicken breast
1 tablespoon of peanut butter
½ tofu burger
12 almonds
7 cashew nuts
3 thin slices of ham
1/2 cups of split pea soup
1/2 cups of lentil soup
3 medium cooked shrimp

Food for Thought

Vegetarians can get their share
of the protein foods group by
eating eggs, beans and peas,
nuts, nut butters, tofu,
and veggie burgers.

Protein of the World

In different countries, people eat many kinds of protein foods.

NORTH AMERICA

SOUTH AMERICA

Some quail is eaten here.
(Canada)

Some turtle is eaten here.
(Caribbean)

Some alligator is eaten here.
(South United States)

Some iguana is eaten here.
(South America)

Some snails are eaten here.
(France)

Some snake is eaten here.
(China)

EUROPE

ASIA

Some tuna sushi is eaten here.
(Japan)

AFRICA

AUSTRALIA

Some fried grasshoppers are eaten here.
(Africa)

Some crocodile is eaten here.
(Australia)

Some octopus is eaten here.
(Italy)

25

Delicious Dairy

The dairy group includes milk and products made from milk.

Dairy products can contain a lot of fat. Too much fat is not good for you, so it is healthier to eat dairy products that are lower in fat. For example, fat free milk or low-fat cheeses.

some very healthy dairy — low fat milk — Milk — yogurt — cottage cheese

some dairy — swiss cheese — chocolate milk — frozen yogurt

some not very healthy dairy — ice cream — milk shake — pudding

Milk Troubles

Cow's milk contains a chemical called lactose. Some people cannot **digest** lactose. It gives them a stomach ache.

These people still need the nutrients from dairy products, such as calcium. However, they must get these nutrients from other foods. Luckily, calcium is found in other food groups. For example, it's in broccoli, kale, oranges, pears, salmon, hazelnuts, and sesame seeds.

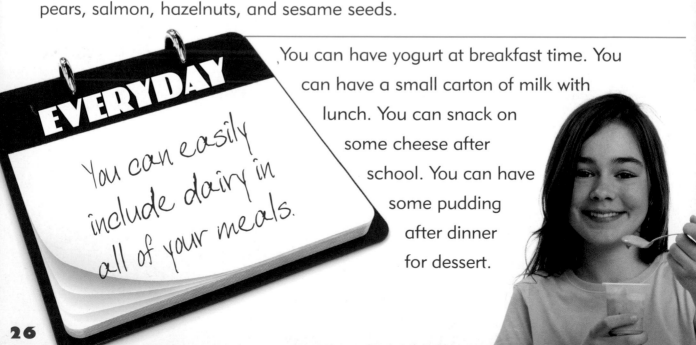

EVERYDAY

You can easily include dairy in all of your meals.

You can have yogurt at breakfast time. You can have a small carton of milk with lunch. You can snack on some cheese after school. You can have some pudding after dinner for dessert.

26

How Much?

Children who are eight years old or younger need two cups a day milk or dairy products each day. Children who are nine years old or older need three cups.

Here are some examples of what counts as 1 cup.

ONE CUP LIST
1 cup of milk
½ pint container of milk
1 cup of yogurt
2 cups of cottage cheese
3 slices of processed cheese
2 slices of hard cheese
1 cup of pudding
1 cup of frozen yogurt

Food for Thought

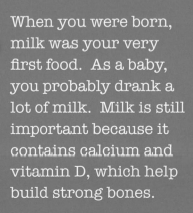

When you were born, milk was your very first food. As a baby, you probably drank a lot of milk. Milk is still important because it contains calcium and vitamin D, which help build strong bones.

Dairy of the World

Around the world, many animals provide milk for people to drink.

NORTH AMERICA

SOUTH AMERICA

cows
(North America)

goats
(South America)

Fruits | Grains | Dairy
Vegetables | Protein

sheep
(France)

reindeer
(Scandinavia)

moose
(Russia)

horses
(Mongolia)

donkeys
(China)

yaks
(Tibet)

EUROPE

ASIA

AFRICA

AUSTRALIA

camels
(Ethiopia)

water buffalo
(India)

Oils are OK

You will not find oils on MyPlate because oils are not a food group. However, you do need a little oil in your diet every day.

some nuts with oils — cashews, walnuts, almonds

some seeds with oils — pumpkin seeds, sunflower seeds, flax seeds

some fruits with oils — avocado, olives

some fish with oils — sardines, tuna fish, anchovies

some vegetables with oils — corn, soybeans

EVERYDAY

It's easy to get the oils you need.

You can sprinkle some seeds on your breakfast cereal. You can have a peanut butter sandwich for lunch. You can eat a handful of nuts for a snack. You can have dressing on your salad at dinner.

How Much?

Children ages four through eight need 4 teaspoons of oil every day. Children ages nine to thirteen need 5 teaspoons of oil a day. Most people do not put foods onto teaspoons before eating. So here is another way to figure out how to get the oils you need.

1 teaspoon equals about:

7 almonds
5 hazel nuts
6 cashews
9 peanuts
8 large olives
¾ tablespoons of margarine
1/2 tablespoons full of peanut butter
1/3 tablespoons of vegetable oils like olive oil,
    sunflower oil, and soybean oil.

Food for Thought

Even though oils aren't on the MyPlate, they are still an important part of a healthy diet. They help your body grow. They are good for your heart, your blood, and your brain. They provide vitamins and help you fight disease.

Empty Calories

There are many foods that belong to food groups, but don't belong on your mealtime plate.

One example is donuts. Donuts belong to the Grains Group, but they are still not a good food choice. Here's why.

They usually are made from refined grains. They usually have a lot of extra sugar. They are usually cooked with a lot of fat.

Sugar and Fat

Sugar and fat helps make foods taste good. But just because something tastes good, doesn't mean it's good for you. Foods with lots of sugar and fat are called "empty **calorie**" foods. They may fill you up, but they have very few nutrients.

Furthermore, if you feel full you won't have room for healthier foods at mealtime.

Other examples of empty calorie foods are:

Candy
Cakes
Cookies
Pastries
Sodas
Ice cream
Sausages
Hot dogs
Bacon

Food for Thought

Today, 9 million kids ages six to nineteen are overweight. Being overweight means people have more fat on their bodies than is healthy. A lot of that fat comes from choosing foods that are calorie empty.

Top Ten Tips

Here are some tips to help you stay healthy:

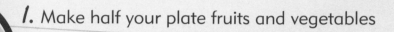

1. Make half your plate fruits and vegetables

2. Start your day off right with a good breakfast. It will provide your body with the energy it needs to get through the day. One healthy breakfast could be a slice of whole grain toast, a hardboiled egg, a glass of low-fat milk, and a piece of fruit or some 100% fruit juice.

3. Choose healthy snacks. Instead of potato chips, eat an apple or some sliced carrots. Instead of a candy bar, have a handful of raisins, a few whole wheat crackers, or a cup of yogurt.

4. Try not to eat foods with a lot of sugar, such as candy, cake, cookies, and donuts. Sugar has hardly any nutrients — no vitamins or minerals. Sugary foods can fill you up and leave little room for healthy foods. Too much sugar can harm your teeth and lead to **cavities**.

5. Cut out soda. Most sodas have lots of extra sugar, and many have caffeine. Caffeine is a chemical that is not healthy. It makes your heart beat faster. It can make you jittery and nervous. It can give you an upset stomach. There are many healthier drinks such as water, low-fat milk, and 100 percent fruit juice.

6. Cut down on fried foods like French fries. They have a lot more fat than food that is broiled or baked.

7. Remember to eat foods from all the groups.

8. Keep your food portions moderate. Don't supersize!

9. Eating all your meals is important. If you skip a meal or go without food for a long time, you can feel sleepy, hungry, or tired. Then you might eat a sugary treat to fill you up fast instead of eating something with more nutrients.

10. At mealtime, chew your food well and do not rush to get finished.

Food for Thought

Your body is busier than any factory on Earth. It is working day and night, week after week, year in and year out. When you follow the MyPlate guidelines, your body will have all the nutrients it needs to get its work done.

B·I·T·E

The choices you make
About foods that you chew
Can lead to a stronger
And healthier you.

I hope that by now,
It is perfectly plain
Why you need vegetables,
Protein, and grains.
And let's not forget about
Fruits, nuts, and seeds
Which give you the nutrients
Your body needs.

Foods that are healthy
Make you a winner
At breakfast and lunch
At snacks and at dinner.

The better food choices you make,
the healthier you will be.
Here is a four-step plan to help you
decide what to eat. I call it B-I-T-E.

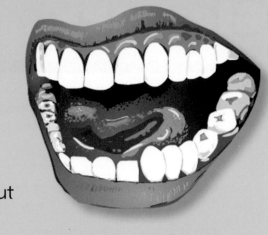

B — Before you choose, think about
what would be healthy to eat.

I — Imagine how good you will feel
about making a healthy choice.

T — Take action. Eat the good, healthy food,
or sip the healthy drink.

E — Enjoy the taste and feel proud of yourself for
making a good choice.

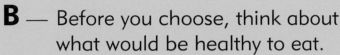

Food for
Thought

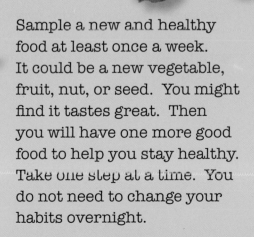

Sample a new and healthy
food at least once a week.
It could be a new vegetable,
fruit, nut, or seed. You might
find it tastes great. Then
you will have one more good
food to help you stay healthy.
Take one step at a time. You
do not need to change your
habits overnight.

37

Glossary

Words that occur in the glossary are printed in **boldface** type the first time they occur in the text.

calorie — a measure of how much energy you get from food

cavities — holes in teeth

cells — tiny units that are the basic building blocks of living things.

chemistry — the scientific study of what substances are made of and how they change

combination — individuals or groups joined together

digest — process that breaks food down into nutrients and waste products

germs — tiny living things that can often cause diseases

infections — sicknesses or diseases caused by germs

nerves — special cells that join together and carry signals to and from the brain

transports — carry from one place to another

variety — a collection or number of things that are all different from one another

Index

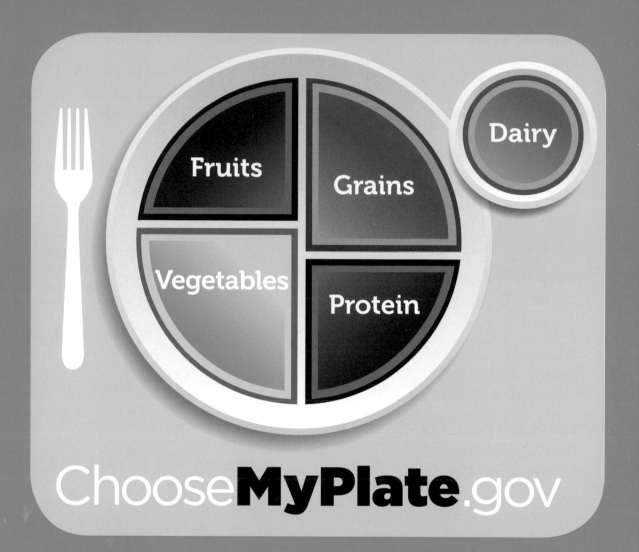

Choose**MyPlate**.gov